DAVID J. MURRAY

Black Hole
and Other Poems

iUniverse, Inc.
Bloomington

Black Hole and Other Poems

Copyright © 2012 David J. Murray

All rights reserved. No part of this book may be used or reproduced by any means, graphic, electronic, or mechanical, including photocopying, recording, taping or by any information storage retrieval system without the written permission of the publisher except in the case of brief quotations embodied in critical articles and reviews.

iUniverse books may be ordered through booksellers or by contacting:

iUniverse
1663 Liberty Drive
Bloomington, IN 47403
www.iuniverse.com
1-800-Authors (1-800-288-4677)

Because of the dynamic nature of the Internet, any Web addresses or links contained in this book may have changed since publication and may no longer be valid. The views expressed in this work are solely those of the author and do not necessarily reflect the views of the publisher, and the publisher hereby disclaims any responsibility for them.

Any people depicted in stock imagery provided by Thinkstock are models, and such images are being used for illustrative purposes only.

Certain stock imagery © Thinkstock.

ISBN: 978-1-4620-7318-4 (sc)
ISBN: 978-1-4620-7320-7 (hc)
ISBN: 978-1-4620-7319-1 (e)

Printed in the United States of America

iUniverse rev. date: 1/28/2012

Contents

Introduction. 1

Poems in a Lighter Vein   5

I a Secret Vampire Am. 6
A Soft and Silly Man 8
Am I Normal?. 9
My Favourite Name 10
My Favourite Place 11
My Favourite Movies 12
My Favourite Scene 13
My Favourite Food 14
Good Intentions. 16
Vanity 18
Party Animals 19
Sounds 20
Flowers 22
Saturday Night 23
Rustic Chivalry 25
A Country Ballad 26
Fools! 28
Awakening 29
Beauty. 30
A Lingering Search 32
Love Song for a Mortal 34
The Millstream 35
I and Thou 36
The Undead 37
Seduction 39
Springtime Again 40

You, Miracle. 42
Making Sense of It All. 43
Carnality 44
Chance 45
Comparing Thee 46
A Poem about a Poem. 47
Identity Crisis 48
Aging 50
Existing 51

Black Hole   53

Drunksong 54
In a Garden 55
None but the Brave 58
Lamplight 59
Explosion 60
Implosion 61
On a Train. 62
Trying Not to Hurt #1 64
Trying Not to Hurt #2 65
The Romance of Science. 66
A Wandering Wish 67
In a Restaurant 68
Sentences 70

Treading Water   71

My World of Words. 72
A Rap on the Knuckles 73
A Fear Renewed 74
Sometimes. 75
Movies and Thee 76
Your Body is Your Toy. 77

In the Sunlight	78
Sad Revels	79
I Have No Portents	80
A Dreadful Mathematics	81
Amity	82
On a Foreign Beach	83
On a Foreign Table	84
On a Foreign Sofa	85
On a Foreign Path	86
On a Foreign Clock	87
On a Foreign Poet	88
What I Must Do	89
On a Friday	90
At a Hotel, Alone	91
Every Thought You Have of Her	92
Compulsive Repetition	93
Breakdance	94
Degrees	95
Too Strong a Dedication	96
Cold Breeding	97
Probability Theory	98
Some Strange Winds	99
A Silent Figure	100
Hopes	101
Re-Reading	102
Glumness Unlimited	103
Am I Caving In?	104
Lake-Blur	105
The First Brown-Red	106

Bagatelles   **107**

Introduction

The topic of romance has been at the centre of most of my earlier books of poetry. *Confusion Matrix and Other Poems* (2007) was less focused on that topic than the others, but the long poem at its start did deal with an emotion that is almost always associated with the start of a new relationship, namely, confusion. In *Surface Tension and Other Poems* (2008), which was openly autobiographical, I described how, after certain vicissitudes, I met Esther Mongrain, whom I married on July 5, 1972. In *War-Wise and Other Poems* (2009), the second section included a set of rhymed sonnets, each of which dealt with some facet of romantic thought encountered in everyday experience. *Celebrations and Other Poems* (2009) was written as a memorial to Esther, who passed away on February 5, 2009. *Persistence and Other Poems* (2010) is certainly the darkest volume of the series, dealing, on the one hand, with an early romance ruined by inexperience, and, on the other hand, with a tension-fraught romance with somebody who was highly experienced. My most recent volume, *Pursuit and Other Poems* (2011), dealt with two romantic extremes; one was an unplanned suicide attempt, fuelled by alcohol, while I was trying to hang onto a long-distance relationship; the other described how I became infatuated unexpectedly with somebody when there were a number of extraneous factors that made my pursuit of her somewhat untenable.

An important word is missing from the above paragraph, namely, the word 'power'. The present volume attempts to get to grips, both autobiographically and philosophically, with the role played by power in romantic relationships. At present, marriage practices around the world range from highly male-dominated (and, often, barbaric) societies to far less male-dominated cultures where domestic abuse is illegal and divorces and common-law relationships are widespread.

In my own rather restricted academic career, the most striking demographic shift has been the fact that, when I came to Canada in the 1960s, male graduate students far outnumbered female graduate students in the Department of Psychology at which I taught. Now, in the second decade of the twenty-first century, exactly the opposite holds. Women are becoming empowered in academia and other workplaces. In this book, however, little will be said about empowerment matters determined by sociopolitical and demographic trends. It is more concerned with the role of power in sexual relationships, and the context is necessarily restricted to the last 30 years or so in Western society.

Power relationships between the genders have been the object of comic plays (e.g., Shakespeare's *The Taming of the Shrew*), comic operas (e.g., Mozart's *The Marriage of Figaro*), comic films (e.g., Laurel and Hardy's *Sons of the Desert*), and, of course, stand-up comedy (e.g., mother-in-law jokes). The first section here, 'Poems in a Lighter Vein', describes the everyday hassles associated with being a vampire. A vampire cannot go out in daylight, he cannot see himself in a mirror, and garlic is extremely noxious to him. Yet, as I was writing the thirty-five poems in the order here presented, I could not help finding myself moving from comic misadventures to a more voyeuristic obsession with the fact that a vampire exerts power, not only over ordinary humans in the streets and fields, but also over his many 'brides', women who never age or die naturally and who are predatory in their search for new recruits into their bridedom. I found myself unconsciously yielding to caveman-like fantasies about 'having' as many women as a vampire might have; these fantasies might be permitted to be embodied, as many fantasies are, in the field of fiction as opposed to nonfiction.

The second section, entitled 'Black Hole', contains 13 serious poems, each of which can be interpreted as a description of, or comment on, the role played by power-hunger in relationships. All of the poems, from 'Drunksong' to 'Sentences', are about the coercive power men can wield over women. For example, 'Drunksong' deals with the latent megalomania that surfaces in a large number of males when they are in an advanced state of 'problem drinking' and are seriously drunk. 'Implosion' is indirectly about how easy it is for an otherwise well-meaning male to get a 'power kick' by leading a female on, making use of his native talents, and then unexpectedly dropping her, even though he knows he is wrong to do so. The two poems entitled 'Trying Not to Hurt' describe the near-impossibility nowadays of *not* hurting somebody, given an atmosphere in which 'dating' several partners at the same time is conceptualized as a possible preparation for marriage, or as an end in itself. The three narrative poems entitled 'In a Garden', 'On a Train', and 'In a Restaurant' are all based on events I actually experienced, either in Canada ('In a Garden', 'In a Restaurant') or in England ('On a Train').

The third section, 'Treading Water', is about one particular issue that can be found throughout the animal kingdom and the human realm: namely, rivalry between two males as to which one can exert the greater power of attraction on a particular female. Although this section contains 35 poems, not all of which mention rivalry explicitly, the reader can assume that even the relatively harmless 'I wish you were here' poems written from a foreign location all have a restless undertone because the writer knows that while he's away, his rival has easier access to the female in question.

The final section consists of 36 rhymed couplets ('distichs'), a verse form associated particularly with the Latin writer Martial (ca. 40–100). The verse form was revived by Goethe and Schiller in a magazine they edited in 1796, where the couplet form was used, scathingly, to answer some of Goethe's and Schiller's critics. Here, I have called each couplet a 'bagatelle' because one meaning of that word is 'a piece of music in a light style'. Beethoven wrote three sets of bagatelles for solo piano, throw-off pieces, so to speak; the 36 bagatelles of the present collection are meant to sound trifling, but they are also meant to arouse deeper thoughts surreptitiously, something one might not expect from poems of such brevity.

Again, I am deeply grateful to Rachel Breau, M. L. I. S., and Marissa Barnes, MA, for their help with manuscript preparation. I am also grateful to the editorial evaluation staff, the copyeditor, the proofreader and the design team assigned to the book by iUniverse during its production phase; I would particularly like to thank Brian Hallbauer of iUniverse for his continued interest in, and encouragement of, my work.

Poems in a Lighter Vein

I a Secret Vampire Am

I a secret vampire am
and nobody knows but me.
I descend upside-down down castle walls
and take haemoglobin with tea.

I wander the waiting graveyard wastes,
howling in blood-inspired revelry.
I hear how my howls are picked up by the owls
and carried far outward to sea.

I wake when the festive blistering sun
beds himself down, while I flee
from its rays till the moon comes out
and softens with moonlight each tree;

and then do I smile through my toothy fangs
and join in the moonlit *mêlée*
where the moonlight makes magic of commonplace things,
and I search in the moonlight for thee.

O my bride of bad dreams in glittering white,
posed in a halo of moonlit glee,
thou showest the blood on thy fangs to the moon,
then glidest to sit on my knee,

where I know I must guard my very own throat,
keep it safe from thy dentistry,
so eager art thou to find a nice vein
or a lusciously plump artery.

As thou sit'st on my lap and at me look'st
ever so hungrily,
hoping thou'lt taste the tang of my blood
and discover what men-vampires see

when they look at their brides in their moonlit white
while the brides plead an endless plea
that their husbands not drink from them at night,
but search out new members who'll be

people quite willing to have their blood drained
and their souls turned to vampires whom we,
in our turn, will admit to our rollicking group
in a rollicking party and spree

where blood-fangs meet blood-fangs and all night long
'bite', 'drips', 'swallow' and 'gulp' are the
sounds that waft sideways athwart the tombs
while the moon shines dispassionately.

For moons know that suns grow, fizzle and fade,
but vampires go for eternity,
unless they've been lured into sunlight by
spoilsports devoid of vampempathy.

A Soft and Silly Man

Once a soft and silly man
didn't believe the rumour I
was a vampire; he said I seemed to look
too nice to have the evil eye;
but I will catch him by and by
and drink him till he's dead and dry!

Another silly man there was
who didn't believe that I could be
a vampire; he said I seemed to look
too young to know eternity;
but I will catch him by and by
and drain him till he's dead and dry!

But once a girl-child saw me fly
with silent wings and swishing swoosh
across the moonlit evening sky;
I'll catch *her*, maybe, one fine day,
and she'll agree to be my prey.

Am I Normal?

I could go on forever and ever
pretending that I felt super-clever
because I can fly and turn into a bat
at the flick of a feather or drop of a hat;

but really I don't feel quite that way.
I just feel I'm normal, and might even say
I feel an impostor or maybe a lush
because I'm aware that I can't really brush

my fangs; you see, I am forbidden
to look in a mirror, so I have hidden
my crestfallen ego far behind
a persona of being normal and kind.

But simmering there, in my deep undermind,
is the knowledge that I must forever be blind
to how my fangs look by night or by day;
it's only my brides who ensure I'm okay.

My Favourite Name

I'm very glad my name has never been
Crazy Horse;
but, of course,
no vampire ever wanted to be seen

without a name like Nosferatu, or perhaps,
in the vernacula',
Dracula;
not to be named like this would collapse

the heart of any aspiring vampire-bat.
But, all the same,
I'm glad my name
has never been Bonzo or Jehoshaphat.

My Favourite Place

Oh, let the wild winds whirl
throughout my habitat!
No vampire in the world
can ever better that!

Oh, let the wild winds howl
about this precipice!
No vampire in the world
can ever better this!

Oh, let the wild winds race
about these battered trees!
No vampire in the world
can ever better these!

Oh, let the winds wail on
over the thorny roses!
No vampire in the world
can ever better thoses!

My Favourite Movies

Although the mists do tend to swirl
wherever movies make me go,
I'll have you know,
they never make *my* hair to curl;

and though dark crypts and gloomy trees
appear where movies make me go,
I'll have you know,
they never make *my* blood to freeze;

what *does* curl my hair and freeze my blood
is that movies *never* make me go,
for the sake of the show,
to hotels where the beds are soft and the food is good.

My Favourite Scene

I stood at the top of a cliff-top's height
and spread my wings out to the pearly moon.
Daytime would come sometime in the night,
but I hoped that its coming would not be too soon;

for there, as I saw what I saw there below,
I knew what I saw was by moonlight made;
a light can make dazzle of what's but a glow,
and a shadow a blackness of what's but a shade;

so dark and light, dark and white, light and black,
white and black, criss-cross the valley's floor;
I sweep my great bat-wings forward and back,
and feel further forward than ever before.

"Power! Aha! Look, Ma! No hands!"
was the song that I sang from the o'erarching heights
of my solemnmost Ego, down to the lands
of the bold forest-floor in its blacks and its whites,

and heard the re-echo of its strains
pushing and panting over the trees
and off into natural landscapes and plains
like a vocal gust that has turned to a wheeze;

and, as I exulted, flush with my powers,
I thought I heard moonlight that praised me aloud
and thought I saw angels who plied me with flowers
for being more than a face in a vampire-crowd,

for being a vampire ethereal, strong,
a god among bloodsuckers, pounding my wings
up there on the cliff-top all night long,
singing the songs that a psychopath sings.

My Favourite Food

Although I like to scale the heights
of my castles and palaces steep,
I far prefer to penetrate
the throat of a person who's fast asleep;

he never wakes up, for I take great care
not to rattle the bed or to ruffle the air.
I always come in by a window I open;
I never come in up the stair,

for stairs can creak or betray me by
the clomp of my oncoming tread;
and I always avoid the bedside table
for fear I bump into the bed.

I even take care to bring Kleenex along
in case of a glugular vein;
so I drink up my fill and I quietly leave
making sure I have not left a stain;

and the person wakes up with a stretch and a yawn
and sees in the waste-bin a tissue
he thinks had blown in, through the window ajar,
but nothing else seems like an issue

until to the bathroom mirror he hies
and notices dots on his neck;
"Did *I* do that shaving?" he wonders aloud,
and answers "I probably did, what the heck";

while I, on the roof of my victim's house,
see it's time I must be on my way,
for the cockerel's crowing, the cattle are lowing,
and the bumblebees buzz at the break of the day,

to the dank of my coffin and cold of my crypt;
but I'll tell you a secret, so please bear with me:
The person I bit, as he now eats his cornflakes,
doesn't know that he'll soon be there with me.

Good Intentions

I wandered lonely as a cloud
that floats on high o'er vales and hills
and wondered what on earth was meant
when lawyers talked of 'codicils'.

It is a clause they add to wills,
changing the dead one's legacy.
Sometimes the living think them daft
and doubt the deceased's capacity;

and sometimes the living, unlike the dead,
think ill of the codicil's goal;
I'm thinking now of a man I once knew
who tried to bequeath his very own soul

to his cat, to ensure its survival.
Contested it was, that codicil,
by all who had known the man and his pet;
they testified that they loved the man still

just as much as they'd loved him in life;
but, before he lay mouldering in his grave,
he'd known that neither kinsfolk nor friends
to look after his cat would dare to be brave;

so, to save his cat's soul, he had given to it
the soul he had owned himself throughout
a life where he'd mainly thought about work
and all that he'd had to go without.

So he'd left his soul to his only cat,
assuming his soul would help it to thrive.
It was then that I heard of his codicil
and decided to make his corpse come alive

to see how he managed without the soul
that had gone to the cat when the lawyers had won;
I made him stand up, in his open-pit grave,
with his arms waving mildly beneath the moon,

and noticed he seemed to have nowhere to go,
for he suddenly tumbled down to the earth
like a toppled philosopher who had learned
his ideas had been greeted with mocking and mirth;

for a cat has a feeling a human does not;
for felicities feline it yearns;
for angelical harmonies nothing it feels,
nor sings 'Many Happy Returns';

so the soul of the cat rejected the soul
of its owner; I caught its remains,
as they shot from the cat, in expurgative jet,
in my cloak, where I still see their stains;

and, slightly bemused, I got on with my life
(I mean, death) while the stars stood on high,
and the daffodils bloomed but a few days each year,
and I'd learned to let sleeping cats lie.

Vanity

I think that I shall never see
a vampire lovelier than a tree—
unless, of course, that vampire's me;

for, in my bathroom mirror, I can see
nothing whatever of little me,
nor can I see a single tree.

Hence we are equal, I and the tree,
because, in my mirror, we both are free
of visibility.

Party Animals

How could you know that I'm planning to throw
a party for my peers?
Vampires will fly from all parts of the sky
to sample my bubbling beers.

From here and from there they will soar through the air
in ultra-vampirical finery;
and they'll come down to earth, in the land of my birth,
at my Transylvanian winery.

We will then hold a ball and invite one and all
in the village to party away.
They will dance cheek-to-cheek for the whole of a week
in a spirit of innocent play;

and none will suspect that their lives will be wrecked
when we bus them all off to a glade
where our fangs we'll bare in the moonlight's bright glare,
and sgrazoom! one and all will be made

into vampires like us with a minimal fuss
and with brand-new fangs for no fee;
and we'll then pass a night giving maximal fright
to all the drunk drivers we see.

Sounds

Sometimes I glumly and gloomily sink,
on pinion'd bat-wings, down to the ground,
in order to solemnly brood and to think
about whether I really enjoy *any* sound.

Sights I can bear; my eyes grow wide
at the thought of a beautiful nape
on a beautiful girl who might serve as a bride
and from whom I would never attempt to escape.

Tastes I can stand, and I crave fresh blood
whose pungent aroma reminds me of home,
and I feel my nostalgic emotions flood,
and I know a quiet tear to my eyeball will come.

Smells I can like, save for garlic's dark pong,
that has me wondering all through the night
if I had done something terribly wrong,
when humanoids munch it with unfeigned delight.

Touch, oh, ah, yes, I like the feel
of the wind on my wings as I softly land
on the westernmost wall of my castle and steal
handfuls of stonedust to harden my hand.

But sound … what is sound? And why is it there?
A sound gives to me, almost always, a fright;
I'm afraid that my footfall makes others aware
of my shadowless presence outside in the night;

I'm afraid that a twig-snap will give me away,
or my silence at bedsides be spoiled by a burp.
No, sound you can keep while I keep it at bay;
and I daren't use a straw to silence a slurp —

the holes that I make with my two-sided bite
are too narrow for straws to be utilized there;
so I drink pianissimo as long as I might
till I've finished my drink and fly off through the air.

Flowers

Oh, what a nuisance flowers are!
Just when you're getting all comfy and sleepy,
somebody brings a bouquet to your graveside,
and the smell of dead tulips is horribly creepy.

The scent of dead roses can even be worse,
and marigolds, mouldy from mildew and weather,
are something akin to a gravedigger's curse
as they mingle their odours and stenches together.

Nettles smell better than buttercups, yet
a wreath of narcissuses, jonquils, and phlox,
with tincture of frond baby's breath can upset
your composure more than can hollyhocks.

That's why, I believe, our forefathers of yore
gave up sleeping in graveyards and took to the habit
of sleeping in coffins, though it cost a bit more,
but at least they were free of the smell of dead rabbit.

Saturday Night

When it's 'Saturday Night at the Movies' on TV,
that's really inconvenient for me,
for my victims need time ere they stumble to bed,
not quite right in the legs, not quite right in the head,
and they keep me up waiting, outside in the rain,
while they run to the bathroom and back again;

and even when Morpheus, God of All Sleep,
is sick of their counting of countless sheep
until they drop off, and he passes me by
with a nod of the head and a wink of the eye,
I know he will know that I don't stand a chance
of drinking their blood if they opt for romance;

so, one dark night, I stole their antenna,
an act from the bowels of a vampire-Gehenna.
I waited while they smoked and drank for hours
till they drifted upstairs to their separate bowers,
and when the sounds slowly arose of their snores,
I crept through the window and opened their doors.

How beautiful she looked, the Household Queen!
She slept with her cat, but, alas, it had been
scratching with claws at her neck, so she wore
a muffler thick, ten feet long, maybe more,
coiled up around her shoulders and neck, and I
was so miffed that I thought for a moment I'd cry.

So to Hubby's room next I wended my way;
I could feel in the distance the breaking of day;
I looked out through the window to see if a bat
could fly safely; but I trod on the cat.
The darned thing scratched me, right through my cloak,
and the husband awakened and sleepily spoke:

'What is it then, diddums, did Mommy forget
and has not put your food and your water out yet?'
And I froze in horror in case he saw me,
but he went back to sleep, and that feline Banshee
jumped up on the bed, headed straight for his throat,
and wrapped itself 'round it as if to gloat.

Frustrated, I turned to escape ere the dawn
would floodlight the bedrooms, the house, and the lawn.
I flew like a flittermouse, dare I say?
And got back to my castle ere breaking of day;
but over and over again I'll malign
television, before which I'd always done fine.

Rustic Chivalry

Just where a weeping willow wept,
at the side of a countryside river,
I once met a girl who was proud she had kept
her promise to meet me, 'her demon lover'!
'neath the boughs of the tree, for a rendezvous,
an evening tryst—but the wrong thing to do;

because when she sat down on some grass she had swept
clear of pizza-box bits and of beer-cans galore,
I endeavoured to calm her and make her accept
that I'd thought they had cleared it the day before,
but, now, I went on, I would set her aflame
by being the 'bat guy', and live up to my name;

but I pulled the wrong ripcord in my mind,
and turned into a werewolf raised as a pet;
to my doggie devotion my date was blind,
and, throwing a stick and shouting, 'Go, get!',
she called me an irresponsible worm
who could never be trusted again to confirm

that I was the man that she'd thought she was getting.
She'd thought I'd regale her by drawing her blood
with my two-pronged fangs in prolonged blood-letting,
while she'd be my girlfriend, as she'd understood;
but all that she'd got was me begging she pitch
more sticks in the river for me to go fetch!

So off in a huff she went, hat in her hand,
away from the willow, away from poor me,
and I knew that I'd be there for a quite a long stand
before the spell vanished and I would be free
to transform myself back to that thing of the night
whose blood-dripping fangs she'd described as 'all right'.

A Country Ballad

> *No one can guess the doubles I've seen;*
> *a bat that's a man and a man that's a bat*
> *and a bat that's a woman and a woman that*
> *a bat would have been if…*

Maisie was a pretty girl who lived by the village green.
On Sundays and on holidays, she obsessed with thoughts obscene,
but on weekdays and on work days, on sick days and days off,
she behaved oh, so politely that she'd never even cough.

But came the holidays and wow! What *had* got into her?
She'd smile a little smile like a joke had just jumped into her,
but she'd tactfully look away when dogs and cats went at it,
and the strongest oath she ever swore was 'Drat it!'

Because, you see, according to a widely mongered rumour,
she'd met a vampire who'd possessed a viral sense of humour,
who, instead of into her neck with famed precision biting,
had bitten into her upper arm 'because it's more exciting'.

But Maisie was a lady with a well-developed sense of principle,
if she could have a life so long that she'd become invincible,
then surely the things worth living for would multiply and grow,
and the only things she lived for were vampires on the go.

If only she were one of them! But why, you ask then, wasn't she?
Hadn't she been well bitten, with a vampire's hot intensity?
But you should have marked the gist of my words above:
I said he had a funny bone beneath his bites of love;

for he had, in that bite on her arm, injected into her
a vaccine against vampire bites; it trickled into her
like arbitrary pinpricks; *her* soul would ne'er be borne
to a vampire vale from which she'd ne'er return;

David J. Murray

and she would never have a chance of creeping out at night
from a home-based coffin she'd made her own, and might
upgrade to a condo-coffin should the money come her way,
but in the meantime she'd have been quite content to stay

young! Ever young! Oh, how the night birds call
as they watch the bats snatching the insects off the wall
to fill their alimentary tracts with all they need
to properly digest the blood on which they feed!

But none of that for Maisie; for her the moonlight's glow
might merely mean that tomorrow it might snow,
and blood for her was nothing but a nuisance and a chore,
an everlasting nosebleed that was nothing but a bore;

and mirrors never would be sign of something supernatural;
she'd only see herself as dandruff'd, hair up in a ball;
or acne spotted every time she wanted to go out,
and even when she smiled at herself, it looked more like a pout.

Garlic was just a tasty thing that other people ate;
shadows were things beneath your eyes you got if you stayed out late;
and human beds had nothing like the charms of stone or wood.
Beds were just places children were sent who'd not been very good.

All was a dazzling mockery of what real vampires had,
and Maisie got so angry that she started being bad,
putting bedbugs into honeymoon suites in all the best hotels,
and climbing into steeples to silence wedding bells;

and thus did Maisie prove my point: what might have been
was only what it might have been had not that vampire seen
how funnier it really was, or were, to decimate
all Maisie's hopes of vampire life and leave her to stagnate.

Fools!

When colours come and force their way upon you,
as they do when long days of rain finally yield
to the coming out of the sun from behind the clouds,
and poets spring up out of every corner and field,

I, vampirical, laugh and look down on them, fools!
It's only the night steals Arcady from the moon;
it's only the stars that stir scatter-dust about
the black that constitutes the Night's dominion;

it's only the moon that, slyly, like a girl,
flutters moonbeam eyelashes while I grow
my bat wings like proud angelic outerparts,
turning my batness into a hero below;

and so, laughing, I climb the castle walls
to spread my giant wings (though their shadows never loom
on the moonlit dustlight scattered o'er heath and hedge)
and pour out, onto humans, my prophecies of doom!

Awakening

I can awaken what the Kraaken feels
as dimly through the deeps it steals
waiting to pounce on drowning men
and take them into its regimen;

but the Kraaken brings people unto death;
I give them life with my vampire's breath
and the slow lust lingering of the thrill
that draws them ever closer to the kill.

Like weepers are vampires, crying inside,
humanity's monsters with teeth bared and wide,
as we churn through the sea or the pitch-black night
keeping our victims forever in sight;

for Nature is red in the vampire's tooth
and the Kraaken's great claw in the depths underneath,
but his leads to nothing but Natural Law,
while mine leads to Nature herself in the raw.

Beauty

Ingratiating flattery batters me,
but does not get me down.
It shows I'm human if the words
of someone, who respects renown,
are uttered with a sophistication
I savour in my appreciation.

And yet this flattery places me
in a distant space; I am not one
of them, mere humans, who display
their limits to the rising sun,
while I take cover while it's light
until the fall of the following night;

but then! I can change to a vampire bat!
Or a werewolf! I'm most certainly not
a human crawling on this earth
bemoaning all his sorry lot,
wishing he'd been genetic-made
to live his life in moonlit shade;

but, one day, I caught a humans' bus,
which some of us use on busy days
when the humans grow lovesick beneath the stars
and yearn into our eyes to gaze;
and there on the bus was a youngish teen,
showing her legs as she stood between

my seat and where others stood on the bus.
I tried not to stare, but focused my mind
on the pentatone scale and the Golden Section
and places where silvers and golds are refined,
when she pulled out her cell phone, which had rung,
and talked rather sharply, as if she'd been stung,

to the caller. I jerked my head up, was curious;
and looked into eyes that formed pillows of bliss,
hazel and liquid they were, feeding hope
that one day I'd re-know a feeling like this;
I moved my eyes downwards, avoiding her knees,
back into thinking of Socrates.

My mind had been pulled and had been caught up
by a tiny pool of a teenage affection
but didn't dare plan any furthering more
that would forge with her a stronger connection,
vampire with human, age with youth,
too rich for a vampire who's long in the tooth.

A Lingering Search

When cities and towns conspire to weep
for fear of me, I start to brood,
wondering whether the vigils I keep
ever blow anyone any good.

It's nice to be feared, yet I know, deep inside,
that it's only a renegade foil to keep out
the nice guys whose competence addles my pride
and rivals who care not what life is about.

So I sharpen my fangs and practise my howls
and polish the nails at the end of my wings.
Ere parting at dusk, I empty my bowels,
comb my fur, and anoint me with ointments and things.

I make sure that I've locked up my castle securely,
and check all the lights are out ere I depart
on my lingering search for those walking demurely,
a give-away sign that a woman has heart,

and thus is a victim to take for my bride,
a beauty to savour that very same night,
a woman who'll show every inch of her pride
and insist she be given a trousseau in white.

Meanwhile, there are dreamers who sit and who mope
in the darks of the forests and shades of the fields,
folks who've lost faith and all vestige of hope,
folks o'er whom Fate its sorcery wields.

She'd show them the bridal gown *I* had had made
when I gave her her freedom to live on and on,
and to find, in the quiet of a woodland glade,
some dreamer deliberate who had gone

to be caught by a vampire like her and pulled down;
the moon through its cloud-river seems to skim
as she bridally presses her prey to her gown
with a blood-soaked grin at her power over him.

Love Song for a Mortal

The air is starting to sag
with the burden of my being;
half-animal, half-human,
I can never be all-seeing;

for the bat-sight catches moves,
the human-sight catches colour.
Synthesis is difficult,
and confusion takes me over;

and when the bat-sight fails
to view the night-sky vast,
and when the human-sight misses
a movement that has passed,

only confusion clouds my head,
and the only thing that's true
is that my vampire's animal-self
wants to be human like you.

The Millstream

I heard a babbling millstream brook
that put me in mind of a number of songs,
contained in a well-worn music book,
where lovers wrangle beside the stream,
and the river's the place to sigh and to dream,
and to drown in and thereby to right all your wrongs.

But I am a vampire and stronger than most;
not for me is a dump-death of hapless *amour*,
or a Severn-deep tavern death at the cost
of a savage book-taking of all the arrears
of lost rendezvous, mishaps, and indolent tears,
and *faux pas* that no Cupid would ever endure.

No, I'm strong in the moonlight, the cave, and the crypt;
no woman can ever make *me* weep, I'll get to her first;
I'll upset Romance with a brand new script
where I'll meet all resistances with a jeer,
rebuff all rejections with flair and good cheer,
and calm all my anguish by slaking my thirst

on a potbelly surfeit of wine and strong beer,
not to mention a beautiful neck, slim and round,
that I pierce with my fangs when I'm close up and near
to enjoy the smooth warmth of the red of her blood
(unaware that she's giving it 'for my own good')
and then sink, with a satisfied smirk, to the ground.

Thus this is agenda, a conquest-delight;
all my brides I'll parade in a long procession
that winds 'round the graveyard one beautiful night,
while I silently giggle on top of the tomb
I am sitting on, multiple groom,
a vampire who has achieved full possession.

I and Thou

Although a human is allowed to say
that all the clouds have gone away
(at least for an hour till they all come back),
a vampire can still say the same, as well,

because, at night, when the moon is high,
a cloud can move across it in the sky
so only a feeble glow remains
of the moonlight's full effulgent spell.

So what's the difference 'twixt him and me,
or her and me, who are trying to be
writers portraying the Universe?
Nothing, so far as I can tell,

except that humans have a fuller
Universe that is richer in colour
than mine, which hobbles along in the dark;
but mine is nearer to heaven than hell.

The Undead

A stubborn cast of adjectives reclaims
the follies of the undead, and their names;
but nowhere is stated with whom those undead slept,
their brides-in-death, whose names were secret kept,
while brides-in-life, while named, might go unwept.

Love is a force that grippeth even me;
when I look at the summery waves of greenery
that wave in the forest winds, I look to catch
any young lady whose throat looks ripe to snatch,
and who, perhaps on purpose, may detach

herself from the sprawl of my wings and raven cloak
as I move in hungrily; to her it's a joke
if my bat-winged wing tip touches her on her shoulder,
for then she can even try to fan the smoulder
of my greed, emboldening me to be bolder.

Or maybe a milder Sunday-school kind of lass
will see me coming and move to let me pass,
not realizing how my claws are itching to grip
her soft white arms and invitingly narrow hip,
thinking I'm merely a bat-man out for a Sunday trip.

Or maybe an older woman has had her fill
of pretending her honeymoon's present still
although it's not; she stands for a type of undead
who'll compensate in Death for the life she'd led,
being Queen of a Vampire Prom in vivid red.

But little equals the strong and vibrant force
when the unrequited undead seize their course,
once I have given them Death; at first, they fuss
with poems, but soon a sidestream ominous
of unrelieved sadness grows, till, mutinous,

they *want* their bridal names carved into stone;
they want to live forever, but *not* unknown;
they scream that Love, with a violent capital L,
and an omened O, and a V that casts a spell,
have an E for an Ending they hope is all well.

So, reminiscing, I look at the forest-tops' waves,
lazily swishing the trees that tower over the graves.
Here are the undead, those who have left their tomb,
for an active vampire life of varietal bloom,
except for those brides who still weep for an Unknown Groom.

Seduction

I do not burn the midnight oil
at any kind of desk;
instead, I churn and reel and roil
in midnight's glow as on I toil
looking for those, who, at my behest,
will wriggle with joy at being my spoil.

The moon shines bright on my crazy sport
as over the branches I fly;
only the dawn-up can cut me short
as I fly, wanton, to escort
any young damsel who would like to espy
what I keep in my castle and crypt and court.

Blood I thee offer by taking it out
from your arteried body so soft.
As it drains in my mouth, you will shout
at the joy you have found in its outwards spout
and your soul will mount me-wards aloft;
and when you are free, you will be in no doubt

as to whom you will give, on a midnight clear,
all that your loving can ever bestow;
as you stand by your gravesite, free of all fear
save of daylight, you'll know you are near
the fount of all blessings here below,
a regimen blood-loss you'll always revere.

So come, gentle children, come fly with me
to my castle of poison, my homeland of death,
where you will stand, indissolubly free,
by the cavernous coffin where you will now be,
waiting to breathe your unending breath
on us both in our boisterous ecstasy.

Springtime Again

Where the green carpet of Springtime climbs
to stifle the browns of the branches grey,
I watch and gauge it as if the times
were right for new victims to lure me their way.

I look down from my castle at the trees,
searching for movements on the tracks
that thread, muddy and stony, to tease
the wayfarer onto their puddles and cracks

where he or she each hopes to find
an outplay, rigorous, plentiful, free
for the growing yearnings of his or her mind
for Nature, which — don't be surprised — means me!

So I watch each movement, each tiny burst
of colour of blue or red of a coat
on the track of a human who, at the worst,
fears only a trip on an oversized root.

Not once do they think that they're at home
in Nature as well, a part of the green,
and the blinding blueness of the dome
of the sunlit sky; they walk between

the tall straight trunks of the pine and spruce,
happy to not have to wear too much.
They never expect the pain abstruse
that I cause them when I promise such

a bite of Death as benefits forever.
But I must wait till the sun has gone
before I swoop; for I must never
forget that humans care not to walk at night.

But this whole poem, released from my pen,
is logical slapdash, for I quite forgot,
that I *can't* look downwards from my den;
I *sleep* in the daytime; these lines are rot.

You, Miracle

The miracle you were in daily life
is propagated afterwards past Death.
The white you wore in Life to watch the spring
propels itself on forward in the sheath
of bridal white you carry as the wife
of me, your vampire husband and your king.

And more than one of you there are, out there,
brides for a fang-rich glutton for their blood;
into the freezing crypt I watch you glide
perpetuating into death the good
I wooed you with to lure you to my lair,
where I can watch your movements, filled with pride

of ownership, in this my animal realm,
where power and lust combine to overwhelm.

Making Sense of It All

On how many worldly numbers have I spent my time
trying to make sense of a Universe where Nought
is a number and where square pegs never fit?
Oh, what a relief it is to see the night
with her beautiful spangles and her infinite
casts of moonlit shafts no painter ever caught
and her unlimited promises sublime!

I look out at the night from my battlemented tower
and see in the forest-glades below what no men
or human women know exists, a revelry
of my bridal wives, helmeted with desire,
waiting for me to charm them with my deviltry,
to cast them into wanting of my acumen,
to furnish them with tastings of my power!

I'm freed by what superiority
does to my ego-strength, and shed no tears
for those humans, weighed with their worryings
and uttering petty songs to ward off grief;
I feel complete when I watch their scurryings
hither and fro to mollify their fears
while I am free, for Death is my priority.

Into my death I go, where, arm in arm
with slender-armed women dressed in white,
I shall progress from avenue to avenue
of new addresses, caves, and graven tombs
where every place is a place where I can do
all that I want to pleasure and delight
my bridal bodies who *desire* my charm,

and who, in responding to my beckoning,
become the soul survivors of life's reckoning.

Carnality

Carnality falls in real life where it will,
but, in my freedom to stalk through death's abode,
I have carnality wherever it appears,
in wood or vale or solemn highest hill.
All I need do is go there with a bride,

a slim one or a plumper one in white
all dressed as for a bridal life-in-death.
I know she'll be responsive down the years
that hold her new life riveted to a night
that fills her strengthened lungs with endless breath.

So on I go, appraising my new life,
sundered from living by barricades of black
that fill my tomb when the sun begins to set;
then start I up, and caress whatever wife
happens to be waiting as I wake

and call 'surrender!' to the evening's red,
and rise to walk the moon-enshrouded road
that leads me to Nature, where I quite forget
the miseries of my human life; instead,
I straddle the Night as Colossus once bestrode

the harbour where the sea glittered with fire;
I straddle the path that through the moonlight leads,
out to a place where worldly dreams beget
impossible pleasures only dreams inspire,
dreams that are always upstarts from misdeeds.

Chance

As though the folds of darkness folded more
than did the soft black pleats of the night,
I felt a darkness fall across my mind
although the moon was shining fullest bright.

One tiny accident, one unintended fall,
that could prolong my earthly life till Day
rose in the dewy morning and its beams shone full
on my resting visage as concussed I lay,

could bring an end to all my happiness,
could bring an end to all I had enjoyed,
could render a long and lasting testament
of fidelity to my brides to null and void;

and they would wander lonesomely, coldly,
looking for one who'd wined their glowing veins
with his joy, but was no longer living,
his corpse corrupt and rotted by the rains.

Comparing Thee

Can I compare thee to a summer's dawn?
No, no, my bride, for summer dawns are death;
the light they spread across the Eastern sky
forecasts a tomb of deadly death descending,
while I, in a frozen state of fear, head on
to face the Day's mortality of death,
and, worst of all, the loss of lovely Thee,
blessed in Thy bridal veil, stained
with the wistful nectar and beloved mead
of a red-filled blood that to Thy beaded white
lends vehement nourishment, *Thy* sign of Life;
so I must never compare Thee to a dawn,
but to an evening fine with skeinèd silk,
pretty and bright to greet the oncoming dark.

A Poem about a Poem

'A terror-striking vehicle of death am I;
my footprints stink like lead-pits in the sky.
When the sky rains and the ugly clouds on-merge,
I lead the charge up to their very verge
to send the rains of death down to the earth,
and watch, maliciously, at the unmagick'd birth
of floods, where swollen worms and smelly smells
rise from the water as it swirls and rolls and swells.'

All that was a poem that spat out from my pen.
Violence have I within, for I'm not at one with men;
where they lie low in storms and winds and hail,
I spread my point-finned wings as I regale
the storm with a sense of urgent unity
and praise it with a nightingale immunity,
and wince as I look down on weak humanity
in its nightly throes of sleepless near-inanity
in a world where men and women don't possess
what I have in my Vampire-land, no stress
because of inequality; I share
with all my brides blood-borders free of care.

Identity Crisis

Am I some retrograde re-visitation,
some ancient sparkle from some ancient block,
ancestor questing the future through bloodlines and pedigrees,
a scion of some dark moronic rock?

I look around as the winter starts cementing,
pouring its hesitant ice on cliff and crag,
steering the sun down a staircase of luminous darkdom
as off I start on my evening's jugular jag.

Night in the winter is only pleasing
to owls and to hunters from the north;
I take no pleasure in feeling I'm freezing
when off on my blood-jag I sally forth.

My brides stay home and congeal there;
less welcoming are they, less smile.
The fire in their hearth crackles upward,
but its smoke hovers heavy a while.

No patience have we with a worship
of somebody higher than us;
we go on our own ways our own way,
and banish all worshipful fuss,

for we know eternity always,
because we survive year on year;
we muffle our fangs in our quiltings,
and stomp on, to stomp out, all fear;

And onward we roll unimpeded;
forever our lives avoid death.
We hover both northward and coldward,
but never run out of cold breath;

so, like a retrograde warrior,
I stand as the winter creeps on,
king of the vampires, but servant
of Daylight's dominion.

Aging

And my verses grow colder and colder;
I cannot bequeath them more warmth.
I want to act bolder and bolder,

and churn out mystery plays
wherein the actors brusquely
complain of the sunshine's rays;

but a force like a weeping detracts
from any such masterpiece;
I shiver within at the facts

that I dare not be caught in a net
of human narcissism,
nor can I dare to set

a trap to entangle a human
in the hope I'll be able to segue
my soul into that of a woman;

so my verses grow colder and colder;
I cannot bequeath them more warmth.
Even immortals feel older.

Existing

By dumbly marching two by two
into the ark,
the animals didn't leave a place,
in its dark

for one creation, peering in—
a vampire, me,
who spreads his bloodlust through the world
promiscuously!

So never do I ever march in time
to any band;
I and my wives spread, ravenous,
over the land,

and spread our news of a midnight life
everywhere.
A moonlit sonata always plays
where'er we are,

and yet we're cast a-down with doubt
because, you see,
we'll never know how to taste your kind
of sanity,

where reason is caught like a modest dream,
pure and real,
and conversations are just what they seem,
and just how they feel;

but in our world of vampire power,
all we know
is how to entice and captivate,
in moonlight's glow,

victims who yearn to leave the Day
and flee
to where the midnights swoop and play
unendingly.

Black Hole

Drunksong

Where the wild posy grows
and the alcohol flows,
I shall bury myself in the sea;
and when night throws its pall
over those I enthral,
I shall stand, high, erect, full of me.

Though the stars turn to wine
and the sea turns to brine,
I shall always, in all ways, feel free;
so let posies blow wild
over woman and child:
I shall always, for always, love me!

In a Garden

A tiredness blunts my mental mind.
A garden is where one hopes to find
relief from the torments of the day,
an eyeful of colours in glowing display,
proof that the world still possesses retreats
where a person can ponder his hopes and defeats.

We'd tilled that garden and pulled up the mint
that was spreading its ravaging roots with no hint
of the flavour it gave to juleps and lamb.
Each pull was a dig-and-push-pull (or a 'damn!')
overlooked by our neighbour who, since he'd retired,
had watched, from his garden, how others perspired.

But soon it became his time to go;
it was spring, and the ground was free of snow.
We had helped him relax in his final days,
but, now that we'd parted our separate ways,
it was time for our garden to brandish new flowers,
with no neighbours to watch how we sweated for hours.

So a six-foot fence with a trellis on top
was built round our garden. Now we could shop
at garden centres to purchase supplies
for its flower beds, now shielded from neighbourly eyes,
while clematis grew up the fence, each a vine
that, once at the top, blossomed petals divine.

The widow next door soon moved out of the place
they had rented for years, so new renters would grace
(or disgrace) that old house, which was never forsaken.
A lease on that house would often be taken
by recently marrieds, some who had children,
and needed the space of a house with a garden.

Of all those husbands, one drew my attention;
neat and clean-cut, he drew no dissension
from me when we spoke in our short conversations.
I liked him quite well, and had few reservations
on how he'd behave as acquaintance or friend.
'Good fences, good neighbours' does not offend.

And his wife was a prize, nicely normal and pure,
with a pleasing demeanour of bold and demure;
but on gardening, neither was notably keen.
As the afternoons shortened, I forged a routine;
every day I examined my clematis' growth,
but I never saw him or saw her or saw both.

One day, in my house, I heard, from the back
of their house, a shouting as if an attack,
an offensive, were moving palpably near.
Listening hard, it was easy to hear
how the shouting from him eclipsed talk-back from her,
till their voice-noises dimmed to inaudible blur.

And then, some days later, as sunlight arrayed
our garden with afternoon shadows and shade,
I suddenly saw, through the trellis's wood,
how, out in their garden, somebody stood;
the wife was outside, but she either stood still,
or walked slowly as if she were going to be ill.

Then, I heard how her husband yelled drunken abuse;
from their window I heard she was 'no bloody use',
with a welter, a windfall of words so unkind
that escape must have been the main thought in her mind.
But then she saw me, at the fence, at my haunt,
and considered I might be her confidante.

But, once at the fence, she had nothing to say;
I tried to send thoughtstreams of comfort her way.
I thought of inviting her round the fence
but knew that her husband would then take offense.
The physical danger was only too clear;
but courage, I saw, underlay all her fear.

Days later, I saw that her parents arrived;
at first they had figured her fear was contrived,
but when, in my presence, *my* worries they'd feel,
they instinctively knew her dilemma was real,
so they all left the house and the house was re-rented;
I never did learn if the husband repented.

None but the Brave

None but the brave deserve the fair,
and so we all idly tear our hair,
we young ones in a world where the old
get garnered granaries of gold.

None but the fair deserve the brave,
and so they dig their layered grave,
the blondes with flashing shiny men
who'll get them, then move on again

to further fields of greater power
while the ugly and the limping cower
in quiet deep caves of melted ice,
wallowing in their avarice

and need for beauty and repair
in a world where only doctors care.

Lamplight

So pale and unrelated are the fates
of the dark and non-effete
to those of 'normal' women
that the woman on the street
holds her dark knowledge tight
and never says, to anyone's ear,
what she thinks about at night.

Thus shrouds the moon's pale light
even the lamplight's shade,
while the paving stones show a sheen
an evening rain shower made;
these glistening lights do not reflect
her fantasies, because she has to be
taciturn and over-circumspect.

Explosion

Meet a mind that's met its death
on a harlot's paid-for breath;

the dream of a wanton wedding night,
everything working, everything right,

coming together in glad surprise
that poets sing when they rhapsodize

on the coming together of two as one
in glad enraptured union —

all *that* was shot to a shrivelled shred
of a vanished dream in a harlot's bed,

and, while I looked at her paid-for lips,
and leaned too hard on her paid-for hips,

the clock ran on for evermore,
for I was learning to love a whore.

Implosion

My self-revulsion is my rot;
I try to be pleased with what I've got,
when all I feel is a sympathy
for him who thinks he thinks like me.

I see no evil, but run away;
I hear no evil, though I play
music that surges from inner sin
and calls the hearer to come right in.

I speak no evil, unless this line
evil betrays by saying 'I'm fine',
if evil be pleasure when others weep;
often it's best, one's silence to keep.

For power is a rotted gateway to a hell
wherein good men are far too prone to dwell.

On a Train

'It's hate that makes the world go round'.
That ought to have been a final line,
a punch, in a poem designed to mine
the fervour of a mind unsound.

But no, it's here first because it's a fact
that I first heard these words, which were shouted aloud
by a Brit, on a train, to a full British crowd,
each one of whom heard him, but dared not react.

He laughed at the way that his blatant disclosure
sent shock through all those to whom it was new;
so he showed off again, thereby offering two
provocations to dent our collective composure,

because at his side sat an adult girl,
to whom he had earlier promised ice cream,
but his tone made it clear he'd attained his own dream
of finding a slave-girl for *his* social whirl.

By flaunting her before the whole carriage,
he'd made his mentality clear to us all,
as well as his hope there'd be nothing to stall
what could only turn out as a horrible marriage,

in which he'd be free to torment and to tease
this unfortunate girl who seemed shackled to him,
and in which he'd feel free to indulge every whim
to command and control if she'd ever displease.

The train gave a shudder; it started to brake.
I looked at the girl, and I knew that she knew
that there wasn't a man on that train who would brew,
there and then, any trouble just for her sake.

I had to get off at the very next station.
Silent I'd been; I'd felt trapped in a net,
no melee did I want, or fracas, or upset
that would stop me from reaching my next destination.

And so I did nothing. I simply detrained;
a coward I felt, as did all who had been,
like me, unprepared for what they had seen
or for vigorous venom expressed unrestrained.

Trying Not to Hurt #1

I dream of others as well as you,
but know that I can never do
more than express my dreams in word,
not deed; I feel I am absurd.

And when in the street I see run past
a glorious girl who's running fast
to get past me and get to B,
I let my images run free

of how I'd get her to my bed,
sprinkle orchids o'er her head,
spellbind with roses her anatomy,
and play with her, and she with me,

but now I must try to heed the morning's call
either to think of you only, or of no one at all.

Trying Not to Hurt #2

With your quiet and loud demeanour
suffocating for a dream,
do not let your eyes grow meaner,
or become not what you seem,
for the grass is only greener
where a sunlight true can gleam.

And I must turn my anger
into something I control,
fight against my tropic languor,
fight against my *Doppelgänger*
who halves what is in my soul
into symmetric melody split in two,
one attracted to everyone, and one to you.

The Romance of Science

When Newton watched his apple fall,
he thought of Nat'ral Law above all;
he did not think of guns whose roar
made cannonballs over battles soar
and fall to the ground in parabola.

When Einstein saw his equations grow,
he thought not of 'crosses, row upon row'
in Flanders fields, and probably never
of a melancholic, war-ripped endeavour
that would drop a bomb on Hiroshima.

So, as a psycho who wants to be logical,
I feel it a duty anthropological
to say that science should have the aim
of preserving Shakespeare's 'what's in a name?'
as phantasmagoric enigma.

A Wandering Wish

A wandering wish can never break a stone.
It stands upheld, a millstone on the waves
of the wild unconscious flowing and alone,
alone, alone, that nothing ever saves;

but it will through, and it will burst athwart.
The dam will break, the millstone fall and crack.
Nothing can make the secret wish abort.
Nothing can fight to win and hold it back.

The secret wish that folds and flows through life —
it is the union that brings deep minds to one.
It is not Nature, but the glow of eyes
that, dazzled, peer in one communion;

it is the look that breaks the wish's flow
until it dies away in afterglow.

In a Restaurant

While riding the dying waves of a spouse's lament,
each day to her hospital bedside I silently went,
and often, when she dozed, I'd creep downstairs
for a coffee at the ground-floor restaurant.

One day, I filled my tray and then looked for where
I might sit, preferring a table with nobody there,
and found one, and sat, then saw, at the table ahead,
a woman, oldish, alone, with nondescript hair.

It seemed too unsocial to not give a small fleeting smile,
but her mouth and her eyes returned bitterness, blankness and bile.
I was taken aback, looked down at my tray, and I drank
rather shakily, knowing I'd go, in a very short while,

in a kind of retreat, climbing back up those echoing stairs;
then a man with a tray took me quite unawares
when he sat at her table, facing the woman, his back
toward me. He solemnly started to add to her cares

with a stream of such gloating and non-stopping nagging
that each movement she made showed a draining and flagging
of motive-to-move; but she bore herself bravely,
and ensured that she did what he said in his bragging.

And then came the time they decided to leave for their home;
he stood up, and, allowing his eyes to shiftily roam
over the room, he jumped when he caught sight of me,
for I had been maybe a witness to how this scum

had bullied his wife; but I gazed at my cup and pretended
I'd not heard a thing. So, their terrible snack having ended,
his wife arose with him to tremble her way to their car;
if I'd only been able to follow! I would have intended

to write down its license or make, but, sadly, did not
because duty awaited upstairs; but I never forgot
how big that man's bones were, how heavy and tall his bulk,
a man not to fight with, who clearly had learned how to spot

sensitive people to pester and, not being deterred
by the law or by pity, his malice and motives concurred
when he taunted his victims to tears or despair; by his side,
his wife resembled a tiny weeping bird.

Sentences

In darkness forced to art, a darker mind
finds peace where hate with vicious colouring black
would daub and scorch the masterpiece unsigned.

In darkness forced to music will the rack
of scarred notes enforce the bitter might
to seem more velvet in its dark attack.

In darkness played in verse will all the night
of piled-on anger spill in scales of gold
a wretchedness made redolent of light.

In darkness played in courage will the bold
and quite imprudent man regain his sight
and watch unusual normalcy unfold.

Such words as these show thought replaces look;
each sentence is a foreword for a book.

Treading Water

My World of Words

It's looming up again, my world of words;
you surge in my thoughts again as a brilliant symbol
that life will go on, and that I do not need to question
my craving for the lightness of your fingers,
and the way your eyes tease, from mine, a lingering
longing to lead you. I hear sounds of battle
presented by distant dusk to the gloomy sky,
sighing to silence as evening slips into sleep.

When lines like these foreclose the science-moments,
or acridities of phone-time preparations,
or the putting away of purchases I'd bought
at the shops that lie in wait at the end of my road,
to drop those lines, like mental scrap, were criminal;
those lines are signals that I must fight back.

A Rap on the Knuckles

In the half-brightness of a cool and arrogant morning
I saw a colleague look seriously at me,
while she said that I had made a teaching error;
so I studied her face again, as she looked at me
in my half-dream of that half-experienced morning's
thought, and I saw no harsh adversity,
for she was leading me from the half-morass
of my half-conjectures on reality
to the clarity of the long thought-out insistence
that what is new should always be presented
as a growth from the old. Full buddings should be seen
as sprouts from the same old common vestigial earth
as the old was, but now presented and explained
as if the present arrogant morning threw
an unexpected shade upon that earth,
making the half-bright dark; but that was ephemeral,
because no shadows ever constitute
qualities of anything, just as teaching
can present a truth imperfectly as false.

A Fear Renewed

It is the winter-side of you I want,
the puzzled peerer at historical facts,
the anxious looker at the poorer students,
the pallid occupant of library cubicles,
and beloved wearer of boring winter clothes.

For, when I see the summer-side of you,
a quite magnificent brown left by the sun,
a clearer-than-ever vision of skin,
a happy clatter in your voice when swimming,
these surface as new talents new to me.

And then I feel fear of younger suntanned rivals,
fear that I lose my breath before you do
and must clamber from the pool, abashed
by whatever feelings hide behind your shades,
exactly the fears I went through years ago.

Sometimes

Sometimes the dark can brighten up the night;
a slowly setting sun can skim the clouds
off from the looming night and make it lighter.

Sometimes a tender image shakes the dark;
when all the world seems foe or accident,
an image of a touch makes the contrast starker.

And sometimes an image makes a matter clear;
a knockabout joke can send the mind a breath
of sudden truth wherein a touch seems dearer.

Movies and Thee

Of thee I have thought, while movies gallop on
and the TV is overbright because of the sun,
and I think, as I snack on cashews or ice cream,
how you once shared this sofa in my dream.

And I want to howl at the stunning absence of you,
but do not; I gorge, instead, on quite a few
more cashews, while the movie gallops on
and its colours grow brighter and clearer as the sun

goes down in a fitful ray of somnolent red
and the night grows darker and darker, and my bed
calls me to sleep, but I dread its emptiness;
this sun, that pales my dreams, is merciless.

Your Body is Your Toy

I do not know if now is time to grieve
or clap my hands in metaphoric joy.
The sun has untied those bonds that rarely leave
our joining minds; your body is your toy

for you to run with or swim with in a pool
or a lake, your arms extended to the sun,
while I, jealous, waver from warm to cool,
because I feel my sporting days are done.

All I can do is acquiesce, again,
to summer's making fools of men who age.
Your pliant arms send radiance to young men
while scruffiness and sweat are old men's wage.

Oh, damn these summer days that tear away
from me all hope that I with you can stay!

In the Sunlight

I like the sun because it greens the leaves
and lends, to black petals, shining armouries;
van Gogh-like, I want to paint the light that weaves
uncluttered lineage through their coteries

of similar coils and stems of mellowed green
that burden botanicals with a sense of lush
and quite unleashèd growth and force unseen,
arbour, equivalent of a teenage crush;

but dare I dare to picture the same with me,
looking to be strong like younger men?
And dare I dare to say the same to thee
as rivals may do with awful acumen?

I like the sun for what it does for trees,
but dread the competition it decrees.

Sad Revels

If half of half the world admits, at last,
a problem with romance and would prefer
to epicure be, or even entrepreneur,
or scholar of an ancient scholar's past,

then do sad revellers of the flesh, like me,
hang a slow head in the face of normalcy,
beat a retreat in a quietened shrubbery,
face up to the loneliness of not being free

to chart, with fingers frayed by art's conceits,
upon the back of a woman, or upon
a keyboard, doleful sad companion
that chronicles the course of their defeats

at the hands of half of half the world; we cringe;
our revels have been driven to the fringe.

I Have No Portents

I feel I have no portents for my dreams;
the silence you bring down upon your world,
its lakes and forests, rocks and clouds and roots,
rivets me through like a knife. If you should go,
my world of fantasy and warmth is lost.
Ice stretches a cavalcade of stone
that all delight eliminates; a dusk
that once would have been hallowed in my verse
is now a symbol of blood on a monstrous flag.
How futile this world would be if you were gone—
I could only describe its hollow frippery,
its seeming unendurability,
in words that would faint from their own emptiness
and starve and fade and vanish and not live.

A Dreadful Mathematics

A dreadful mathematics seethes my mind.
No word has come from you by mail or by phone;
either you've found a pleasure of a kind
quite unexpected, or you now disown

my work, and go to others I resent,
or you are ill. Let pleasure be A, overwork
B, and C an illness represent.
If pleasure be true, and, because of A, you shirk

those of those duties you link to me; or whether
pleasure be true, and you have flown up high
to a phase where you and my rival both together
long to embrace as the nights go swirling by;

or whether your overworking mind's depression
has locked its grip on your workaholic soul,
so that both B and C give full expression
to your desire to flee; then perhaps the whole

of your self is reconciled by A and by B and by C,
working, united, to purge your thoughts of me.

Amity

Here, where swallows swoop like unwitting playthings,
gathering each beach to a nesting-place,
the seagulls screech new fears of new disgrace,

because, where the hope for the soaring gulls had been
to claim clean honour and to fuel incipient joys,
now stands a silent silence, left by noise

that vanished when the callings of the gulls
fell under the swallows' calls of amity,
and tensions fell to equanimity,

and custom, lore, and familiar rules were welcomed;
the swallows demonstrate realities
that hidden powers, and similarities,

can line lines up so right that a standard play
can metamorphose to euphorias every day.

On a Foreign Beach

Oh, thou bloomest distant from me, like the rose
I saw here on a beach on a sea-swept countryside.
The rose-tree and its thorns are hard to reach
without an ankle-tripping trek over stones
and pebbles as round and hard as baseballs; though
I could see the redness, somewhat dull, of the rose,
clearly, I was as fearful of treading those rocks
as I would have been fearful of going to an airport
to fly unexpectedly back to the rose of you.
I'd fear too much your negativity;
you'd say I'd blocked your freedom to be you,
and been silly in persisting in my chase
of you, the most distant flower that ever bloomed
just out of reach, just out of clasp, just
annoyed by my daring-to-try but overdry
polemics, spouted here on a stony beach,
away from the chlorin'd pool you frolic in
with a rival buoyed by your parents' acquiescence.

On a Foreign Table

A slab of paper on a table
is all it takes to quite disable
all thoughts I have of forgetting you.
It calls me to write until I'm through
with my latest fumbling fantasy;

and when I'm finished, it lies just there
on the table at that spot just where
I'd seen it lying, calling for me
to scatter my ink so liberally
across its smooth and flawless face

that what was a blank was now a blaze
of open words in an open praise
of you, away in a distant place
enhanced, like antiquity, by your grace,
but penned into presence here as well.

On a Foreign Sofa

You're here, in my imagination, quite
relaxed on a sofa, with a window's light
behind you fitted with rocks of grey, and grass
of a vividness bright and fervid and green;

the warm sea-air, with its wafted smells and salt,
prepared the ground for the springtime's bold assault
on the senses of those who see, through the window's glass
that is over the sofa where you sit, a scene

so bursting with the light that is Nature's heart
that to see you there just complements her art
that has fitted and festooned the forests of this place;
but then I wake up, for here you've never been,

nor probably ever will be, without some pause
in the way that Nature wields her winning laws.
Perhaps my passion for you has a centre of mass
so stable that Nature *has* to encrown you her Queen.

On a Foreign Path

I have done too much today and now I am tired.
A lecture this morning and questions all the day,
good food and a good film as the evening fell,
and then I walked back, over a path, to where I stay.

At the end of the film, a conversation began,
but during the film, my mind had wandered to you
and I sat on a sofa wanting to hold you warm
but, without you, there was nothing that I could do.

I walked back over the darkening path while Night
onward her darkening cloak over evening drew,
and when I got back to my place of stay, I sat
at my table to write out my heart to faraway you.

The table is round and my chair humdrum and hard;
the night leaves its silent impression where I stay;
my mind is a mix of impressions from that film,
but my longing for you is a yearning that won't go away.

On a Foreign Clock

The clock on the wall says nine o'clock
with a handed display and a tick and a tock.
Ten hours must pass before dawnlight breaks
to reduce my broodings on my mistakes.

This kind of unspecified time is rife
with loneliness to fester my life;
I must not give in to my quiet despair
that you in my love-life aren't anywhere, anywhere.

I must move on, acting and smiling,
with my verses seething there, reviling
the blackness descending on my art
because, in my love-life, the only part

you are playing is that of a Mistress of Doubt
who makes me wonder what 'love' *is* about.

On a Foreign Poet

My eyes were closed against the onset of dark,
thinking of Emily Dickinson I was,
when, in a moment's inattentive look,
I opened my eyes and saw that nighttime was
being chased away by dawn's brighter light
and that an end was coming to the night.

The window showed me rocks and ferns and trees.
I knew that, for you, the only thing I'd bring
was Emily Dickinson to prove to you that she
had changed her mind's incessant jostling
to a condensed concentrate of thought
in which her own redemption she had sought.

Never will love for you be more than this:
To save your mind, I went without your kiss.

What I Must Do

New fall the veils of new oncoming dark
wherein shine lights, poems of thought each one;
I must explore each avenue and spark
and calculate which moon goes with which sun.

I must conclude which end will be which start;
I must ask clearly which artifice to use
to spread the lacquered lingering of each part
of you in verse I hope you'll not refuse.

Shall I bring out the jollity of your smile?
Shall I cry out your sympathy aloud?
Dare I expose, in verses versatile,
exaggerations of the way I'm proud

to shout your humanity in my every word,
not one of which is fraudulent or blurred?

On a Friday

Och, it is Friday, four more days must pass
before I'll see thee again, thou bonnie lass,
whom I dare barely hug and rarely hold;
so my head spins sonnets, green and grey and gold.

Thou art the mortifying master-whip
who, with a smile or twist of lovely hip,
inspires me to expostulations wild,
uncanny echoes of a wayward child.

But you incorporate those powers-that-be
that constitute a worldly mortuary
wherein my longings must a back seat take
to the industry and enterprise that make

my rival confident that you're meant for him,
while I shout shattered screams to the Seraphim.

At a Hotel, Alone

If to thee I am not writing,
life is but a chore.
Even after a heavy meal
when I'm replete and all seems real,
life is but a bore
if to thee I am not writing.

If for thee I am not writing,
no purpose hath endeavour.
Even though a fine bed beckons,
my conscience quietly says it reckons
that I can't be very clever
if for thee I am not writing.

If about thee I'm not writing,
fiction fizzles to farce,
for the only verse that seems real and true
is verse that is focused on only you.
The world is spare and sparse
if about thee I'm not writing.

Every Thought You Have of Her

With every thought you have of her,
you dig yourself in deeper.
Snows cannot climb the ravine's walls
so long as the walls are steeper.

Rains cannot sheet the town about
when rain barrels lie thicker.
Nothing can force a storm to go
except a storm that's quicker.

Each thought that builds on the one before
stiffens a mind's endeavour.
Each thought that cancels the one before
seems to be *too* clever,

but every thought she leaves in me
tunnels into Infinity.

Compulsive Repetition

If thy hairs be wires — but thine are not,
but are of sandspun near-coquettish art
lying across your forehead fringèd-cut
and hanging down your back right to your heart.

Yet in my jealousy I see you struck
with laughter while another holds you tight
and I in an anchor corner feel I'm stuck
just where I was in adolescence-night.

Or I dream dreams of being carnal-raped,
some great symbolic transfer of my lust,
and wake to a window stark with sunlight draped
and sunshine streaming through the motes of dust.

There is light, there is hope, yet this sudden darkness-pain
seems to bring on my hopelessness again.

Breakdance

Break, on the bubbles
of dreams, every thought,
for the air is not sweet
where true love is not caught,

and tie, to the tinsel
of every sweet image,
the lips and the fire
of my true love's visage

and break, on the veils
of hallucination,
the trembling awaiting
of imagination

of all she's got
that I have not.

Degrees

Dichotomies in sex there rarely are,
except degrees identified of desire.
One may feel warmth and affection for the other,
but the other is host to loin-defining fire.

One may want eye-linking only,
the other a leg-linking pleasure;
and so grow indefinite multiples,
none of them easy to measure.

But over them all is analysis
where each holds the mould for the other;
sometimes it's true that the eyes have it;
but sometimes it's true they may smother

the loadings of the loins that force assertion,
embalming pleasure in a womb of fears.
But sometimes submission to the eyes' immersion
will keep alive a partnership for years.

Too Strong a Dedication

Thou hast burdened me with too strong a dedication.
Weight was I, too heavy to shoulder away,
but you burdened me with your appreciation
of what I offered, and your hope I'd stay.

Excuses have I none for breaking love-law,
shouting your praise to you when what I ought
to have said was nothing on what of thee I saw,
and silence kept on what it was I thought.

But when your being swamps my hearth and homestead
with its rightness, and your arms and lovely form
disturb my air and steer me on ahead
to a hoped-for being with you as an ideal norm,

with egos muted in duality,
then, from my burdensome weight, you will be free.

Cold Breeding

With all the cold breeding that goes into thought,
why should a panting seem all I've been taught?
Logic and coolness and social propriety,
aplomb diplomatic and endless sobriety,
are all the things that should determine me;
but nothing but touch and lusciousness
are what determine how I think of thee.

So split am I between my wants,
I feel like a nephew caught between aunts,
one who insists that I be respectable,
the other who knows what for me is delectable,
namely, that I should enbind and hold thee to me;
all else is hollow emptiness.
Desire determines how I think of thee.

Probability Theory

Nothing could I determine was true
except the thought that I'd be true to you
if I were sure that you'd be true to me
should war and mayhem scour the sky and sea.

Nothing could I be sure I knew the less
than how I'd act if you were to caress
another while I watched; my mind would drop
into a hole and never never stop.

Nothing could I be sure I knew the more
than how, by pen and paper, I'd restore,
even though frugally, just a part
of what I'd lost after I'd touched your heart.

Some Strange Winds

Some strange winds advocate a sunset sky
with wheels of circling and wispy clouds
struck at strange angles by the sunshine's red.
This is a sky that only lasts an hour
and yet is decisively striking in one's head.

And, like that sky, implicitly important
beyond the timely boundaries of its truth,
was my phone's ring and the sound of your greeting voice;
silence from you had filled the week before
and another would pass before I would rejoice

at its sound again, an isle in a dead-sea waste
of egregious thoughts and vagaries of taste.

A Silent Figure

And when, in the world, the nicest people fell,
smitten by hurts or disappointed dreams,
cursing the minions of enslaving drugs,
or pacing, misunderstanding all the schemes
that society had erected for the protection
of social morals and familial perfection,

a silent figure looked on, dispassionate.
They had no right to force their minds on hers,
and had no right to force her to conjoin
their unfamiliar thoughts, often of strange kinds,
to the lore of familiar logic that she understood,
a force that pampered Passion into Good.

Silent she stood, hearing the death-watch quiver
as the night's dank cold came on and made her shiver.

Hopes

The clouds are high, likely to over topple,
and, with their darkness, drench the waiting town,
the town where I wait for you to doff and down
the deep defences with which you always grapple.

The sun is high, shining atop the sky,
and dries the living tears each raindrop weeps,
and warms the radiant hopes my own heart keeps
that *you* may warm those hopes up by and by.

Re-Reading

When I re-read, intrepid, what I wrote
when the first faint flooding of extreme desire
sparked me to elevate my every note
of song to you to something that was higher,

I want to shed those doubts that now exist
That maybe my rhymes were hasty, over-strong.
Those very lines leave images that persist
so vividly that to question them seems wrong.

Perhaps I should not re-read my wants and lust.
I should stride forward, futurity at the helm;
I should not let mere ardours overwhelm
this reasoned calm that cloaks me like a dust.

But ardours are not 'mere'; they're quintessential
to any poet of the elemental.

Glumness Unlimited

If amorousness is all it is
cracked up to be, then why is this
encomium written as if it was
a kind of dirge? It is because

the indissoluble verity
of what *did* happen to you and me
was fractionated by the fact
that you're afraid of any act

that crosses the boundary of thought;
you fear you'll die inside if caught
in the arms even of those who've made,
of all you are, a living serenade.

Am I Caving In?

And so I'll stop this treading of the water;
I'll stop perpetually being brave.
I'll stop pretending I am really pure.
I'll stop pretending you are just demure.

And, with a heavy heart, I'll wend my way
to where sweet musics laugh and dolphins play,
and stare, dejected, at my carpeted floor,
where maybe your tender feet will tread no more.

Lake-Blur

I see a lake-blur shone on by the sun.
The sunlight breaks between two cloudy walls,
and whether the sunlight stays, or will be done
in minutes, depends on how the weather falls;

so one long gloom can hang remittingly
over the sea-like surface of the lake,
but it can be broken by a gleam, unbearably
quiet and subdued, as the rays leave and forsake

their virtual fulcrum ethereally near
our sun, and downwards fall and penetrate
the grey-throb mistiness of our atmosphere,
leaving a blur on the lake like a daub on a plate.

Looking at light is like trying to peer ahead
as an angel would who knew not where to tread.

The First Brown-Red

September the third, and the first brown-red
from the hillside stares, isolated
in its green surroundings, poking out
from the shrubs and trees that stand about.

Colours are promised, betraying to all
that nothing is lovelier than the Fall,
when silken colours network the sky
in a harbinger backpack of revelry,

ready to laugh the cold away,
ready to spurn the winter's grey,
ready to dash, like an unfeeling metal,
the brightest of life from each lingering petal;

but what I don't know, when I see that brown-red,
is the depth of the water I've still to tread.

Bagatelles

1. Mornings drag on and on and on
   and a week becomes a Rubicon.

2. The steel of the river grows ever colder
   as the coil of the night sky grows ever older.

3. Tiny are the half breaths of the moon
   as they linger in the hope they see you soon.

4. Each wait is a manacle of Time
   suspended in a corridor of Rhyme.

5. A dark reward begins a lighter dream
   where homilies spill like honey from a stream.

6. Only when fortitude stills the massive wave
   can magnanimity walk us to our grave.

7. Against a smooth horizon's wall of trees,
   a stormy sky's a sword of Damocles.

8. I have no counter to thy narrowness,
   for it, to me, is warranty of friendliness.

9. Where do folks go who think that, when they're old,
   they'll still possess the wherewithal to be bold?

10. What kind of night is one that stretches tight
    over a desert, yet nonetheless feels right?

11. All I can claim is that, if my art be true,
    you'll always know when it was written for you.

12. All I can claim is that, if my art be wrong,
    it was not you who piped the way along.

13. Oh, thou hast draped thy figure near a spot
    where Truth thou hast shown and maybe known it not.

14. A thousand chanting yet mid-river oceans
    dapple the sky with their discreet devotions.

15. A sullen sonority of sound
    anchors your footfalls to a solid ground.

16. Unless I write how you've determined me,
    I am an empty edge, periphery.

17. The sky hangs heavy with a full humidity,
    hangdog concealing the sun's timidity.

18. Although a gentle fold of Night be what I seek,
    tall stature shifts my words from strong to meek.

19. The sky is a lucid limpid lump of grey
    that even storm clouds cannot melt away.

20. Birds chorus loudly in the undergrowth,
    weaving potential patterning to drown us both.

21. Machines that mash up the earth to dirty paths
    inventions are of poet-psychopaths.

22. All confidence falls from the moving mobster's mind
    when he surveys the helplessness of mankind.

23. If ritual intrigues mask the deep copper's bowl,
    it's only to disguise the shininess of its soul.

24. Though moments crowd too fast to see the days
    for the minutes, years also have their ways.

25. You are my dreamer and I am quite content
    to see you as a firmament-fire with best intent.

26. Skies seem to crowd and cormorants squawk and hail
    when the dimming lustre of life starts lowering its sail.

27. No play can actualize the spectre of the Real,
    nor drama instigate a sense of how we Feel.

28. With thee, I climb in my mind, clinging on
    to a hoped-for end where fear has come and gone.

29. Sweet ravings of a non-poetic kind
    stop me from urging myself to be more blind.

30. In these mechanical intricacies, I find
    nurture for body and manna for my mind.

31. Can I press down derangement, so it goes
    to a mindless land filled endlessly with snows?

32. In thee a pulse feel I as 'twere my own,
    because we've each our fancied fears outgrown.

33. I see a life spreading Cordoba on a chart
    as if to diffuse its inkiness into art.

34. A radical infirmity makes one's age
    into dynamic drawback, sacrilege.

35. If all I do here is venerate your name,
    I will not change, and you'll remain the same.

36. But if I can do for poetry what men have done
    for music, then you and I and it will all have won.

CPSIA information can be obtained at www.ICGtesting.com
Printed in the USA
LVOW100350150212

268695LV00001B/2/P